SEARCHER FOR GOD

SEARCHER FOR GOD

The Story of Isobel Kuhn

by
JOYCE REASON

LUTTERWORTH PRESS
GUILDFORD AND LONDON

First published 1963
Second impression 1964
Third impression 1965
Fourth impression 1970
Fifth impression 1973
Sixth impression 1973
Seventh impression 1981

ISBN 0 7188 0875 4

PRINTED IN GREAT BRITAIN
BY MACKAYS OF CHATHAM LTD

CONTENTS

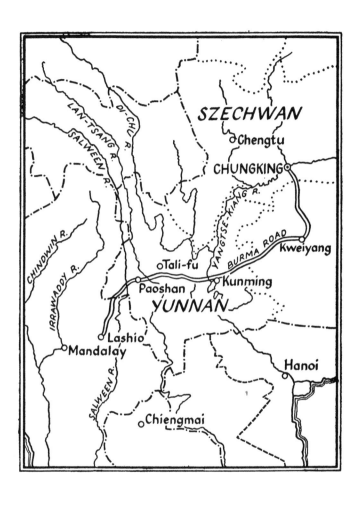

1

GOD HAS A PLAN

"IT'S like this," said motherly Mrs. Whipple. "God has a plan for your life. The point as I see it is—to find out God's plan for your life and then follow it."

Isobel Miller, crouching on the floor by her kind hostess, trembled all over. For years she had been searching for God, trying to be sure that she really believed in Him, and was not just following what she had been told by her parents. Was it true that all this time *He* had been seeking *her*, that her discontent was because she was not following the path He had marked out for her? Her voice shook as she asked:

"Well, how are we to find out His plan for us?"

Mrs. Whipple reached for her Bible and handed it to the girl. "Isobel," she said, "I've always found His will through His Word, this Book. His plan for us will always be in accordance with the Scriptures."

Then the telephone rang and Mrs. Whipple was called from the room.

"So God's plan for my life is in this Book?" thought Isobel, and she let the Bible fall open where it would. How amazed she was to find her finger resting on a verse which gave an exact answer to one question that was puzzling her at the moment! Later, she was to learn that one cannot always get as clear an answer as that—the Bible is not a sort of magic solution to every question. One must also use one's own judgment. But God knew what she needed just then. It was not merely whether or not to go to a certain meeting; it was whether she should yield up her whole life to God.

When Mrs. Whipple came back she found her young guest in floods of tears. They had met only the day before —Isobel was staying with her in Seattle (U.S.A.) to attend a Teachers' Conference—but there was something about this warm-hearted woman that made the girl feel that she had known her for years. Out it all came: her unhappiness in her teaching, her loneliness, her longing to be quite sure of God, her mistakes and blundering. Mrs. Whipple did not ask questions. She let Isobel tell as much as she wanted.

"My dear," she said later on, "this summer we are having a Bible Conference at The Firs on Lake Whatcom. I wish you could manage to come. You would enjoy meeting all the young people and I know it would help you."

Then Isobel, touchy and proud, drew back a little. She wasn't going to be pushed into anything!

"I'm sorry, Mrs. Whipple," she said, "but I've already signed up for a Teachers' Summer School. Until God leads differently, I must earn my living, and can only do it by teaching."

Mrs. Whipple did not press her; but she had a conviction that somehow she must get Isobel to The Firs!

*   *   *

Isobel went back to her teaching in Vancouver (she was

a Canadian, born of Irish parents), and tried to make the best of her work. Then one day she received a letter from Mrs. Whipple enclosing a five-dollar bill.

"This came to me as a gift," she wrote, "and I believe it is the Lord's provision for your boat tickets to The Firs. Won't you come as my guest? It will cost you nothing."

One couldn't just turn down such a generous offer. But The Firs Conference came right in the middle of the Summer School—would she be allowed to go off for ten days like that? She knew that another student-teacher had applied for a week off and been refused.

"Well," she thought, "if it is God's plan that I should go to The Firs, He will make the way plain." She first prayed about it, and then went straight off to see the Registrar and ask for ten days' leave. It was granted at once, without any questions asked! The way *was* plain.

So one evening in July Isobel found herself driving over curving roads through fragrant pine-woods, with two friendly young people who had been sent to meet her. At the house dear Mrs. Whipple received her with a motherly hug, and soon she was sitting on the floor of a big room lit by a blazing log fire, among a crowd of cheery people who made her feel more at home than ever she had been in her life. As the simple service went on she felt at rest, content.

Afterwards she was led down a woody path to the little cabin she was to share with Mrs. Whipple's sister-in-law, Mrs. Edna Gish—and that was for her another wonderful experience. For Edna Gish was the young widow of a missionary, and had just lost her dearly-loved husband in a very tragic way. He had been drowned, in China, while they were on holiday a year after their marriage. But Edna did not let her grief overwhelm her; she had come home to America to recover, and had bravely undertaken to lead the young people's meetings. Living with Edna, sharing a bed with her, talking freely as two young women together, Isobel learned what a life given to God could be.

Naturally, at her meetings Edna talked to her group about the challenge of missionary service, and finally she asked who would offer for foreign service if God should call them.

Now Isobel was not the sort of girl who longed for foreign travel. She did not like discomfort, and she was shy of meeting new people; and as for foreigners—the idea scared her. But she had given her life to God, for Him to fulfil His plan for her. If He wanted her to go abroad, well, of course she would go. How, where, did not matter. Up went her hand.

2

"BUT I'M NOT A MAN!"

A YEAR later, Isobel was at The Firs again. This time it was like coming home. Like a schoolgirl home for the holidays she ran from place to place that she remembered and loved: the quiet place among the trees where she had prayed alone, the open-air meeting place, the big room with the fireplace—and, last, the dear cabin where she had shared such precious times with Edna. Down the path she flew, her brown eyes sparkling, dark hair tossing, threw open the door and was half-way in before she realized that someone else was there. A middle-aged man was sitting alone.

"Oh, I beg your pardon," she stammered. "I didn't know this cabin was occupied——"

He looked up and smiled, and Isobel backed away hastily. "Some old bachelor," she thought. "He looks lonely." And then she forgot all about him in greeting old and new friends, and learning her duties as a waitress— for she was to earn her board by service. But when they gathered for the evening meeting, there on the platform was the "old bachelor" of the cabin!

He was introduced as Mr. J. O. Fraser, an Englishman, of the China Inland Mission. That was all she knew at the time, though later she found out that he was a brilliantly clever man, an engineer and a musician, who could have had a great career in business if he had chosen. But he had been called of God to missionary work, and he had answered.

The China Inland Mission sends its missionaries to the front line, to places where no other missionaries are working, often where no white man has ever been. Mr. Fraser had been sent to the furthest south-west of China, to the mountains where the Yunnan Province meets the Burmese border. Here, perched in little villages high among the mountains, clinging like swallows' nests to the slopes, live tribes who do not speak Chinese, who indeed are not Chinese at all. Isobel could see it all as the speaker described it: the women in their bright clothes with turbans twisted round their heads, jingling with silver bangles and chains of cowrie shells, the lithe men with their yellow-brown skins and bright brown eyes; the terraced rice-fields, the thatched bamboo huts. These people could not read or write—their language had never been written down. They did not worship idols, but their lives were ridden by the fear of evil spirits. Such were the Lisu, the people to whom Mr. Fraser had given his life.

Evening by evening the missionary took his hearers with him in imagination, climbing the steep winding trails to villages which hung over sheer precipices falling into deep valleys; sitting in smoky little huts learning the language, and writing down the sounds—the first time anyone had done so; patiently teaching the people to read their own language from the scripts he had made, so that in time they could have the Gospel in their own tongue; struggling to make them understand the love of God as shown in Jesus Christ, so that they could be freed from their fear of demons and live a new and joyful life. How hard was the struggle, how lonely, and only to be won by constant prayer! And then he told of the tremendous joy when the harvest came, when first a few and then more and more of the Lisu gave themselves to Christ, and here and there little Churches were formed, and the weary missionary, toiling up the rough path, would be greeted by shouts of welcome from the Christians and led to the tiny ramshackle chapel with his own little room behind it—a "prophet's chamber" like the one built for Elisha. At last he spoke of the need for more missionaries; young men willing to live a life of utter hardship for the sake of winning more and more of these people for God.

Isobel listened, and her heart was filled with love for these Lisu whom she had never seen. She longed and hungered for them. They seemed somehow to be in a special way *her* people.

"Lord," she prayed, "I'd be willing to go. Only I'm not a man!"

*   *   *

She had already offered herself as a missionary to China, and was planning to go to the Moody Bible School to be trained. But there were so many difficulties in the way that it sometimes seemed as if she would not get even so far as the Bible School. To begin with, her family were dead against her becoming a missionary—especially her mother, who could not bear the thought of her only daughter going so far away. Her parents were good Christians, but to lose their precious Isobel—that was too much to ask. "Isn't there plenty of Christian service for you at home?" they said.

"Over my dead body do you go to China!" her mother once cried passionately. Isobel felt torn in two.

So she was amazed when she found that her father had invited Mr. Fraser to come and stay with them for a week before he went back to China. "However did he dare?" she wondered. "Mother will not be pleased. But plainly it is part of God's plan for me."

Mrs. Miller was a great lover of music, and Mr. Fraser won her heart by his splendid piano playing, so that made things easier. Isobel waited her opportunity to tell him about her problems, and the chance came when one afternoon she was asked to take him down to the beach (they were staying by the sea on holiday). There they sat while she explained her difficulties: her mother's unwillingness to let her go, the fact that her father had no money to help her through Bible School, and that her brother was out of a job, so that they had been depending on her earnings as a teacher.

"And yet I do feel that God has called me! Or do you think I have made a mistake?" Isobel asked earnestly.

Mr. Fraser told her, "When I meet with obstacles, such as you are finding, I test them in this way. I pray, If this obstacle be from Thee, Lord, I accept it; but if it be from Satan, I refuse him and all his works."

In after years, faced again and again with obstacles which it seemed impossible to overcome, Isobel remembered Mr. Fraser's prayer. She found that any barrier could be broken down, *if it were God's will.*

The wise missionary had more to say. "It may be that even after you get to the Bible School, Satan will try to get you away. For instance, a telegram might come saying that your mother was very ill and urging you to come home immediately. Now, if that should happen, of course you would not be able to leave immediately you got the telegram. You would have to pack your bag and get your ticket. Now, is there anyone where you live whom you could trust to find out the truth and let you know?"

"There's Mr. Charles Thomson, Secretary of the China Inland Mission," replied Isobel, wondering. He spoke so very seriously.

"The very man!" exclaimed Mr. Fraser. "If you receive such a telegram, get into touch with Mr. Thomson immediately, asking him to find out just how ill your mother is. When you get his reply you will be able to tell what you ought to do."

It seemed as though God was showing the future to the missionary, for his warning came true most strangely.

*　　*　　*

Various signs assured Isobel that she was right to persist in going to the Moody Bible School. A friend from The Firs supplied the money for one year; there were ways in which a student could earn enough in part-time jobs to see her through the whole course. So in spite of her mother's grief Isobel set out, across the American continent, from Vancouver in Western Canada to Chicago the great city of the United States. She never saw her mother again.

Mrs. Miller had an operation and died before Isobel could be warned. She could not even get home for the funeral. How sadly she remembered those words, "Over my dead body!" But later she was comforted to hear that her mother had told a friend how she now realized that

Isobel was right to obey God's call, and that she had become willing to give up her girl.

Then came the big test that Mr. Fraser had so strangely foreseen.

It was in December that Isobel's mother died. In January of the next year, soon after she had gone back to Bible School, she was called to the office of the Dean of Women. What could be wrong? The Dean's face was very grave. She held a telegram.

"What is the matter? Tell me quickly!" begged Isobel.

"Sit down, dear. The telegram reads: 'Father fatally injured in elevator accident. Come home at once. Murray.' Who is Murray?"

"My brother. Oh, but I can't stand it! Father too!"

"Is there anyone we can call to help you, dear?"

Suddenly Isobel remembered Mr. Fraser's words of warning. Could it be that this was a plot of Satan to get her away? She determined to take his advice. She had a good friend, a Dr. Page, in Chicago, and she asked him to wire to Mr. Charles Thomson to find out how bad the accident really was. Meanwhile she packed her trunk to be ready—in case.

The answer came back that evening: "Father improving, sends love, and says, stay at your post. Writing, Thomson."

It turned out that her brother had lost his head in his alarm. Her father, though badly hurt, recovered.

3

ROAD-BLOCKS

THE year was 1926, and Isobel was twenty-five. She had graduated from Bible School, now she was to go to Toronto for preparation in the China Inland Mission Candidates' School, before she could be finally accepted as a missionary. Here she would begin to study the Chinese language, and here also the Council would observe her, to see if she were really fitted for so great a task.

The two years had been hard, earning her keep as well as studying, and her health had nearly broken down. It was a thin, tired girl who sat in the train, and a rather anxious one, waiting for the start. Her dear friend Dr. Page—Daddy Page she called him—who had come to see her off, leaned over her comfortingly.

"Don't be afraid, Isobel. There is nothing to dread in candidates' school. The Mission has known you from a child."

No, surely there was nothing to fear. She knew she had done well at Bible School, she was prepared to work hard at her language lessons—it could not be long before she would be on her way to her life's work. And there was another, private reason for her longing to be off.

At Bible School one of Isobel's great friends had been Kathryn Kuhn, also a candidate for China. Kathryn's brother, John, was there too. When John and Isobel met —she acting as waitress in the Institute restaurant, and he washing dishes there!—though they did not even know each other's names, they had felt a strong attraction; such a strong attraction that they tried to keep out of each other's way, in case they should be distracted from their studies. But of course th ey did meet, and love grew up between them, though they would not put it into words. Now John and Kathryn had both been accepted and had sailed for China, but John's letters made it quite plain that he was waiting for Isobel to come and join him. No wonder she longed for the preparation to be over!

*   *   *

First set-back. An anti-foreign uprising broke out in China, and the China Inland Mission did not feel it right to send out any more young missionaries until things settled down. The second set-back hit poor Isobel right in her heart. It seemed so unfair, so downright cruel!

After she had been in Toronto about a month, she was called to the Council for a kind of examination. That evening Mr. Brownlee, head of the candidates' school, called her in to hear the result.

"We were quite pleased with your answers," he said, "and we have liked having you here. But I have something serious to tell you. You know we have to take up all your references—write to the people who have known you and who can tell us about your character. Now I am sorry to say that there is one who did *not* recommend you. The reason given was that you are proud, disobedient and likely to be a trouble-maker."

"Who said that?" demanded Isobel, her Irish temper flaring up.

"That I must not tell you. We are not allowed to betray what is told us by referees. But it is someone who has known you for several years. Now I want you to understand what damage anyone of that character could do on the mission field."

Isobel was hardly able to attend to the wise and gentle talk he gave her. She felt too indignant. Proud? Why, she was ready to make friends with anybody—poor and shabby, or wealthy and charming, simple-minded or clever—just as long as they were what she called "interesting". Disobedient? When she had tried so hard to keep all the rules of the Bible School, even though some of them were tiresome and unreasonable. She remembered So-and-So, whom everyone thought so much of, who broke all sorts of rules in secret because she said they were unreasonable. But Isobel had promised to obey, and so she did. A trouble-maker! Well! She never gossiped or told tales, and tried to be at peace with everyone. Oh, it was too bad! It wasn't fair! It wasn't true!

What was Mr. Brownlee saying? "So we have decided to accept you conditionally. In any case you could not be sent out now, with all this disturbance in China. Meanwhile you must wait, and the Mission Council in Vancouver will watch you to see if you have overcome these faults. If we see that you have done so, when the door opens to China once more, you shall go. We are so sure that you will win the victory," he added, "that we will pay your fare back to your home in Vancouver, as we would have done if we were sending you to China now. It has not been easy for me to say these things."

Isobel rushed to her room with her brain in a turmoil. All that night her mind went round and round and over and over—Proud—Disobedient—a Trouble-maker—who *could* have accused her of these things? And now there was a further worry. If she was not going to China at once, she would have to earn her living somehow. How? Would she have to go back to teaching, harder than ever after such a long gap? What could she do?

Worst of all—what would John think?

The few friends to whom she confided her trouble backed her up. Of course it was all wrong and unfair. She wasn't like that at all. Someone had behaved wickedly, that was clear. Whoever could it have been? It was good to have so much sympathy; but the letter that did her most good was not sympathetic at all. This came from a fine young man who had dedicated his great musical gifts to God.

"Isobel," he wrote, "what surprised me most of all was your attitude in this matter. You sound bitter and resentful. Why, if anyone had said to me, 'Roy, you are proud, disobedient and a trouble-maker,' I would answer, 'Amen, brother! And even then you haven't said the half of it!' What good thing is there in any of us, anyway? We only have victory over these things as we bring them one by one to the Cross and ask our Lord to crucify it for us."

*   *   *

Honest Isobel confessed that Roy was right. She might not have *behaved* proudly or disobediently—but wasn't she being proud when she only took trouble to be friends with people who "interested" her? Wasn't she often disobedient in her heart? Didn't that quick temper of hers perhaps make trouble—or might it not do so if the Lord did not control it? On her knees she admitted it all and prayed forgiveness, and the bitterness was washed away by love. She owned afterwards that this disappointment had really been a great and valuable lesson.

And the "earning a living" problem solved itself—or rather God had planned for this too. Back in Vancouver she was invited to become Superintendent of the Vancouver Girls' Corner Club; a club for Christian business girls who had banded together to serve God, to strengthen their own Christian life, and try to bring others in. It was exactly the work for which Isobel was fitted. The girls loved her, she loved the girls. They were delighted to have a young, pretty, merry-hearted Superintendent whose complete giving of herself to Christ made her a joyous, not a "goody-goody" person; and they taught her many lessons about the life of other people. A host of young women became better characters, several had their lives quite changed, and at the end of those two years she saw clearly that everything had been part of God's plan in preparing her.

When her name came again before the Council in Toronto everyone agreed to accept her, and she was told to make ready to go to China.

She found out later that the unkind reference came from a teacher where she had once been at school, who had tried to get her to spy on the other girls. When she refused, the teacher was angry, and took this mean way of paying off her grudge. Isobel did think of telling Mr. Brownlee of this and so clearing herself; but then she thought, "I won't bother the Mission with it. Why try to make them think I am lily-white? They'd soon find out how earthy a person I am." And she added in prayer, "Dear Lord, how princely of You to let me know!"

4

THE SCUM OF YOUR NATURE!

EIGHT young women on a ship bound for China, all full of ideals, eager to begin their work of soul-winning at last, after the years of preparation; and standing before them an older woman, an experienced missionary, going back to the field after furlough. This was their daily Bible study period, when Miss Paxson tried to show them what to expect when they were really on the spot.

Searchingly she looked into those bright faces. "Girls," she said, "when you get to China, all the scum of your nature will rise to the top."

Isobel was shocked. Scum? But they were all nice young women, real Christians, not raw youngsters either. She herself was twenty-eight, and had been through some tough experiences. What a thing to say about them! She was soon to find out what Miss Paxson meant.

First, however, there was the matter of John Kuhn and their marriage. Dearly as they loved one another, the work must come first. Now the love of the Lisu tribe, first planted in Isobel's heart by Mr. Fraser, had grown stronger and stronger, until she felt sure she was called to serve among the mountains; but John had been interested in quite another part of China. "Tell him," Isobel had written to his sister Kathryn, "that he must

not propose until he knows where the China Inland
Mission will send him." But even as she wrote, it had
been decided that John was to go to Yunnan, the south-
west border province, near the mountains where the Lisu
lived; so that matter was happily settled.

Then, the Mission had a wise rule that young missionaries should not marry until they had been on the
field for two years. John and Isobel longed to be working
together. Isobel would have to spend at least a year in
Language School, but after that, why should they wait?
She was to study in Kunming, the capital of Yunnan, and
John was stationed not far away on the railway line. But
suppose he were to be sent off into the mountains? That
would be very hard to bear.

*   *   *

The things she had feared did not come to pass. She
had a happy year in Language School; and just at that time
the Mission tried relaxing their rule about the two-year
wait. Mr. Fraser—to her great joy he was the general
Superintendent of their district—was disappointed. "Now
Isobel will never learn to speak Chinese properly!" he
said, meaning that as a married woman she would not
have time to study. John solved that by offering to do the
housekeeping until she had passed her third language
examination. As a matter of fact she never did become so
good at speaking Chinese as he was, but then John was
brilliant.

At any rate, married they were, amid the good wishes
of all the missionaries and their friends at Kunming; and
after a week's honeymoon at a pleasant hotel—one last

luxury, paid for by a cheque from John's father—they set off for John's station at Chengchiang. And then Isobel realized that she had not the least idea what missionary work in China really was like.

Although the railway line took them nearly to Chengchiang, as the crow flies, a range of mountains lay between them and the town itself. John had arranged that coolies should meet them at the halt, to carry their luggage, and bring a mountain chair for Isobel. He himself, sturdy and muscular, would enjoy the walk. He described enthusiastically what a lovely trip it would be "over velvety wrinkled mountain ranges, piled up one against another to the skyline, affording deep glimpses into separating valleys where quaint little hamlets lay."

Unfortunately it had been raining hard for days, and the trail was slippery. The coolies carrying Isobel had to go so slowly that before they were two-thirds of the way over the sun had set. Down, down they went, picking their way carefully on the rough path, while Isobel clung to her jolting chair and wondered every minute if they would all come down in a heap, with broken bones, if no worse. At last it got so bad that the coolies dared carry the chair no further. Isobel, tired and aching as she was, must walk. It was nearly dark now, and she could hardly see the path, but with John holding one arm and a Chinese coolie the other she slipped and slithered and jumped and ran down the last slopes on to the plain.

At this point she had a glimpse of beauty, for the moon came out from behind the clouds, and by its soft silvery light she could see the great curve of the dark mountains, and, ahead of them, a shimmering sheet of water, the big lake. Isobel drew a deep breath and thanked God.

But they were not there yet. They had still some way to go across the plain. On the path in front of them a lantern shone—one of the Chinese Christians had come out to see what had happened to their missionary and his bride.

"Courage, Belle!" said John. "He says that my servant Yen-ching has prepared a lovely meal for us—he's been waiting for hours." On they plodded, and came at last to a huge mud wall with two massive doors in it.

"Here's the city wall. They shut the gates at six o'clock, but the watchman knows we are coming and will open for us." Isobel was too worn out to answer. The great gates opened and she stumbled through on to the rough cobbles of the streets. At last they came to a doorway.

"Here we are, Belle! Welcome home!" John picked up his wife and carried her through the door and up the stairs to their rooms. "This is our home! Want to see it?"

"Oh, not tonight, dear." Poor Isobel was completely exhausted. "Just give me a bed!"

"But aren't you going to come to supper? Yen-ching has cooked such a big meal!"

Faint with hunger as she was, the thought of a "big meal" only turned Isobel sick. She shook her head, and sank down on the bed—just boards on a trestle with a mattress on top, but merely to stretch out and lie still was heaven.

"Isn't there *anything* you can eat?" John was worried.

Isobel thought she could just manage to swallow some soup, if there was any. Luckily there was a tin of tomato soup in John's stores—and that was Isobel's home-coming feast.

*   *   *

But by next day she was rested and eager to look round her home. It was just two rooms over the little chapel, and stood right on the market street. There were no windows, but the front and back walls were folding doors which could be rolled right back to give light and air. Only then everyone could look in and see what the queer foreigners were doing—and they did. It was not rude-ness; the Chinese simply do not understand the Western idea of having a place to oneself. If you are not doing anything to be ashamed of, why wish to hide? they argue.

There was a sort of veranda at the back, used as a kitchen, and in two small dark rooms at the side lived Yen-ching and his new young wife. They were to look after the cooking and cleaning. The whole building be-longed to Chinese Muslims, who were still living in the back wing. To do the washing, Isobel had to go down-stairs and through the Muslims' quarters to the back yard where there was a well. Clothes had to be hung to dry over their own veranda rail—and if anything should blow away it was never returned, but seized and used by those below. All this Isobel was to find out in time.

At first she was not at all dismayed by these poor quarters. She knew she must live in a humble way, right among the people, but she did not see why she should not make her home as pretty as possible. She set to work with John's help to paint the woodwork in gay light colours, covered the floor with a mat, spread a green and crimson travelling rug over her big trunk, and set out the pretty rattan furniture they had brought with them. How nice and cheerful the place looked, she thought. But soon she understood what Miss Paxson had meant by "scum"!

"Visitors, Belle!" John called out one afternoon, and clattering up the stairs came a group of Chinese peasant women who were in town for the market. Isobel welcomed them delightedly and showed them into the sitting-room. When she had found seats for them all she began to give them the Gospel message, and was glad to see that they understood her Chinese. They seemed to be getting along splendidly.

Then suddenly one of the old women who was sitting on the trunk blew her nose with her fingers and wiped them on the beautiful travelling rug! A minute later a young mother held out her baby over the new mat. Poor Isobel had all she could do to keep her face smiling and courteous, but she felt sickened. She, who so loved things to be clean and pleasant, had to live among people who had no idea at all of what we call "nice" behaviour! She knew it was not their fault—but what a struggle she had against the "scum" of disgust and irritation.

*　　*　　*

There were so many other things she naturally hated. The peasants were dirty, and they smelled. How could they help it? There were no bathrooms with hot water in their mud huts, and clean clothes cost money; but Isobel was particularly sensitive to bad smells. The peasants were lousy and they had fleas, and Isobel never visited any of their homes without coming away carrying several of these disgusting "biters", if not bugs of a nastier kind. As we have said, she did not enjoy travelling; and a missionary on the frontier has to be always on the go. And Chinese food—the sort that the peasants ate, not the delectable things one can get in a Chinese restaurant in England—turned her stomach.

One day they were invited to dinner at the home of a poor Christian family. It was midsummer, the flies were swarming, and the smell of the pigsty next door filled the little room. When her hostess brought in a big dish full of lumps of pork fat, Isobel wondered if she would faint. "Oh John," she whispered, trying to keep a smile on her face, "do I have to eat this? I know I shall be sick."

With a gracious smile of thanks John deliberately picked up a large white chunk and put it in her rice bowl. But as he did so he said in English, "Wait till she's not looking, and give it to our friend under the table!" This was a mangy, flea-ridden dog, and when Isobel seized her opportunity and slipped the pork to him, he soon showed that *he* enjoyed the unexpected treat that had come his way. Strangely enough, later on Isobel actually came to enjoy fat pork. She found that it went very well with the dry rice and dry steamed corn which were the most usual dishes in Lisuland—when at last she got there.

She had never realized that there was so much "scum" in her nature, and was thoroughly ashamed of herself at being so revolted. These poor good people really had no chance of being cleaner in their habits! But she took it to her Lord in constant prayer, and He helped her to bear it, even to overcome it.

5

SLOWLY WESTWARD

"JOHN, *when* are we going to get to the west?" Isobel had not forgotten the Lisu tribe, the people who had seemed to call to her when Mr. Fraser spoke of them at The Firs.

"I don't know, dear. God will send us in His own good time." John was quite happy working among the Chinese. He spoke the difficult language wonderfully well and he loved the Chinese people. Isobel had come to love them too, but always she felt a restless longing to get to the mountains.

As usual, she took her trouble to her Master. "Perhaps I was mistaken, Lord," she whispered in prayer. "Perhaps you didn't really call me to the Lisu."

John, that loving husband, spoke to Mr. Fraser, their Superintendent. He shook his head. "I doubt if Isobel is strong enough to face the rough life," he answered. "We must wait and see."

But not long after—"Whoopee!" cried John, waving a letter from Headquarters. "Belle, it's come! We are to move west——"

"To the Lisu?"

"Well not quite. But much nearer. We are to go to Tali, which is much nearer to them. We might even be able to make an expedition to them from there. It's like this—there has been Christian work at Tali, but for a year there have been no missionaries there. We are to take over the station."

"Whoopee!" echoed Isobel, and the two young people hugged each other and danced for joy, then dropped on their knees to thank God for His guidance.

Tali would be a position with great responsibilities. Not only was there the regular missionary work, but John and Isobel would have young missionaries sent to them to gain experience when they first came out. There were fewer Muslims than in Chengchiang, so the people would be readier to receive the message—for Muslims are the hardest people of all to convert. And there was a body of Chinese Christians to welcome and support them.

Isobel had learned a lesson while at Chengchiang! She sold all her pretty furniture, determined to start her new life with the sort of solid Chinese chairs and tables that would not easily be soiled. People mattered more than things.

★   ★   ★

There was no Burma Road in those days. Travel was slow and hard (though Isobel used to say that she liked it better than whirling over that dangerous track in a motor truck!). The Kuhns took it in several stages, Isobel mostly riding in a chair and John walking, while their luggage was carried by coolies. At night they would stop at a Chinese inn—often very dirty, but Isobel was getting used to that—and take the opportunity of presenting the Gospel to the villagers.

But they had been travelling for only three days when

Isobel fell ill with dysentery. Fortunately they were near a place where there was an American mission, and a little Chinese Christian nurse, Miss Ling, was staying there at the time. It was fortunate—or we ought to say it was God's provision, for Isobel was very ill indeed, and for three weeks they had to remain at Tsuhsiang. She was still very weak when they were able at last to go on, but she did her best to hide it. Perhaps she hid it rather too well.

On June 28, 1930, they arrived at a village which they were told—or thought they were told—was only three or four miles from Tali.

"Will you walk with me the last few miles, Belle?" John asked. "It's quite early. We shall have plenty of time to get to Tali before sundown. We can talk better than when you are perched up in that chair."

Isobel was quite willing. The road was level and the scenery was wonderful. On one hand rose a great range of mountains, on the other the land, green with fields of young rice, sloped away to the great blue lake on which stands the town of Tali. The villages were prettier than Chinese villages usually are, for they were built of stone instead of mud-brick. Every now and then the road crossed a swift-flowing stream whose clear waters were icy from the mountains.

On they went, on and on. Isobel began to be very tired. Mile after mile and still no Tali! "I thought they said it was only three or four miles," she sighed.

It was only later that they realized that the dialect used there was a little different from what they were used to, and that what sounded to them like "san-si-li"—three or four miles—was really "san-shih-li"—thirty miles!

Isobel's steps dragged more and more, but she would not complain. At last she stopped dead. "John, I can't go any farther."

"But we're almost there—look, here's the gate. Just a few steps more," urged John.

It was no use. Even those three or four steps were beyond her strength. John put his arm round his wife, half-carried her in, and laid her down—on the floor, for there was no furniture in the house! Their coolies had not yet arrived.

"Belle, you're awful!" he complained. "When you say you're through, you just stop. You don't try any more."

"But, dear," came a weak voice from the floor, "I don't say I'm through till I am!"

However, the Chinese pastor heard they had arrived, and soon the Christians had rallied round the exhausted Isobel, made her comfortable and brought her a hot reviving supper. Soon she was sitting up, and presently was able to get to her feet and go with John all over their new home.

Such a change from the cramped dark quarters at Chengchiang! This was a big airy house with a large garden, and they had the companionship of gentle Pastor Li, kindest of friends and helpers. Two happy years they spent at Tali, and there their little daughter was born. They named her Kathryn, after John's sister, Isobel's dear friend.

*　　*　　*

Again the call came—still further westward! Ten days' travel over the mountains was the little town of Paoshan, and a few months before Kathryn was born the Kuhns were asked to go over to join the missionaries there in a special evangelistic mission. It was during the long trek to Paoshan that they had their first glimpse of the valley of Yungping, which means "Eternal Peace". They had climbed a ridge and turned a corner, and there below them the mountains fell away in a steep slope to a lovely little green valley threaded by a silver stream, beyond which the mountains rose again, ridge after ridge, closing in the place like a wall. Beyond the stream was the little market town where they were to spend the night.

But Yungping was far from being the paradise it looked. The people were nearly all Muslims, their hearts and minds firmly shut against the Christian message. When John and Isobel went out after supper to hold an open-air meeting, as was their custom, they were surrounded by hard, stony faces. "Couldn't care less" was what they seemed to say. John felt discouraged.

"I suppose," he said as they prepared for bed that night, "someone will be asked to come here and open this place to the Gospel. No missionary has ever lived here. Well, I'm sorry for anyone who has to tackle this job."

So when, two years later, Mr. Fraser asked the Kuhns to take on the valley of "Eternal Peace" John was quite upset. He had loved the work at Tali, and he had been so successful there. He did not in the least want to be shut up in that small valley among the hard-faced Muslims. For once in his life he was thoroughly resentful.

Isobel felt differently. She had fallen in love with the beautiful valley. It was so much nearer, too, to her longed-for Lisu; and she would be glad to be free from the constant entertaining of travellers which she had had to do at Tali, on the main road from west to east. Not only missionaries, but explorers and hunters had to be welcomed at the Mission, and she had felt that her own missionary work was being hindered. No, she would not in the least mind settling at Yungping. It was a pity John felt so bad about it.

A strange thing happened. The work at Tali had been going so well, but suddenly everything went wrong. The bright eagerness of the Christians became dulled—and Isobel fell seriously ill. She grew weaker and weaker, and a great fear fell on John that his darling wife would be taken from him. As he knelt at her bedside, praying that she might recover, the word of God came in a whisper in his heart.

"It is your unwillingness which has cast this shadow. Are you not prepared to do anything, however you may dislike it, for My sake?"

John gave way. "Yes, Lord, anything You ask of me. I will go, and I will go gladly." From that time Isobel began slowly to recover, and blessing returned to the Church at Tali.

6

LISU AT LAST

JUST ten years after Isobel had felt her call to the Lisu, the Kuhns entered Lisuland. It happened quite unexpectedly, one thing leading to another in the way God so often works.

"Wait until after your furlough," Mr. Fraser had answered, when she wrote again about her great desire. He still did not think she was strong enough.

As they had expected, the people of Yungping were not very responsive. Both the Kuhns worked hard—Isobel visited every tiny hamlet in the valley, driving off the barking dogs, pushing into the dirty courtyards and giving her Message to the women. They were kind and friendly, very glad to see her—but only a few of the poorest and most ignorant had accepted Christ. Though God loves the weak and ignorant as much as the strong and clever, in order to form a Church there must be someone strong enough to take the lead; and so far none such had appeared.

"Perhaps it is not for us to see results," Isobel admitted. "We are only sent to prepare the way."

Then came a letter from Mr. Fraser. "I want your prayers for a perplexing problem," he wrote. He told them that in Lisuland, above the deep valley of the Salween river that cuts through a corner of Yunnan before flowing south into Burma, there were two brave little churches. They were six days' journey apart and had only one missionary couple, Mr. and Mrs. Cooke, to serve them. So the Cookes had separated, Allyn Cooke going to Luda and Leila staying at Oak Flat.

"But I cannot allow this to go on," wrote Mr. Fraser. "Leila Cooke is very brave to stay on in that lonely rough place, but I cannot allow husband and wife to continue in separation. Yet I have no one to send."

John and Isobel stared at one another. They had just lost the baby they had hoped would be a companion for little Kathryn, and their hearts were sore. But now they understood why God had taken the little one. With a tiny baby they could never have dared the hard journey and the rough life; but Kathryn was now old enough to enjoy it all. They wrote at once to Mr. Fraser telling him that they felt God was leading them to the Salween valley.

Mr. Fraser was still not sure that Isobel's health could stand it. "Go in for a month," he advised. "That will be a great help to the Cookes, for Leila will be glad to have another woman with her, and Allyn is having trouble with some chiefs over opium growing. John can back him up."

Yungping would not be deserted, for two young women had recently joined the Kuhns, and Kathryn could be left with them. That was the flaw, for Isobel. It would not do to take the small girl just for one busy month, without a settled home for her. It was hard! Isobel walked out of Yungping with the tears running down her face, for her precious little daughter was dearer than ever since the other one was taken.

*   *   *

But the journey over the mountains, well looked after by her sturdy John, was, she said later, "like another honeymoon". Even when they had to put up in a dirty sooty inn which John called "The Dirtiest Inn in the World" she was not discouraged, for the very next day they would enter Lisuland. She fell asleep in a thrill of joy—and next morning woke up with a bad pain and diarrhoea. It was a return of her old enemy, dysentery.

"Belle!" exclaimed John, horrified, "don't say we've got to stay another night in this place!"

"No!" Belle answered staunchly. "If I've picked up a germ here by sleeping one night, I'd maybe have two by tomorrow. We don't stop for this."

"The hardest climb of all is to come," objected John doubtfully.

"Put me on my horse," said Isobel, "and then all I have to do is to sit on it."

So they started. Up and up the trail climbed, zigzagging back and forth across the face of the mountains, while Isobel clung to the saddle defying pain and faintness. At an empty hut by the track they paused, John lit a fire and made Isobel a drink of hot cocoa—the first thing she had been able to swallow that day. Then again they went on and up.

The scenery changed as they went higher and higher. Rustling bamboos gave way to whispering pines, then to great trees hung with ferns and moss. In their shadow it was cold—cold. Isobel's feet and hands were numb, and her head dizzy. She found it hard to cling to her horse. John watched anxiously, but there was nothing to do but go on. At last, with a plunge and a scramble, the good beast pulled himself up over a rocky ledge, and there they were, on the top of the world! Now they were in warm sunshine, and Isobel began to feel better.

"Look, Belle!" John cried, pointing down into the valley. "Down there is a big farmhouse where we can cook dinner. And see, over there, those mountains beyond the valley. That is Lisuland! Tomorrow night we shall be there."

Down and down to the farmhouse, rest and a good meal. In spite of her weariness, the exercise and fasting had done Isobel good, and she was able to eat. Indeed she felt almost well.

"Let's go on to the next village," John urged. "It's still early and the weather is lovely. Our host the farmer says it's not far."

Isobel was quite willing. The further they got that day the sooner they would be in Lisuland. But alas, once again John had misunderstood the dialect, and Old Nest, the next village, was much further than they thought. It came on to rain. Isobel had packed her raincoat in one of the loads, and soon she was drenched. It was seven in the evening before they arrived at Old Nest village, but there they had a wonderful welcome in a big Chinese house. Hot tea and a delicious Chinese meal made her a different person, and soon she was chatting to the women while John preached the Gospel.

The last day's journey took the whole long day, and it was nightfall before they reached a little town on the banks of the Salween river, called Luku. Here three important chiefs had their Yamen—official houses—fortified like castles. Walking with John under the brilliant stars,

Isobel looked up at the dark peaks and thought herself in "Storybook Land". Then on the dark mountainside broke out spots of golden dancing light—the fires of Lisu villages far above them. They had arrived in Lisuland, but they still had to climb up to the remote village where Leila Cooke was living alone.

"She has not seen another white face for months," Mr. Fraser had said. "What a heroine!" thought Isobel; but the time was to come when she could be just as much alone and in far greater danger.

★ ★ ★

The Cookes lived in a thatched bamboo shanty just like the ones the Lisu villagers built, but Allyn Cooke had laid out a fine garden in which grew plenty of vegetables. Isobel fell in love with the place at once. To be sure it was a rough, camping sort of life. The Lisu villagers were every bit as dirty and flea-ridden as the Chinese peasants. They had practically no furniture and ate their meals off a board on the floor, where the dogs and cats could help themselves! The living-quarters of the houses were upstairs, and underneath the cattle were penned, which meant smells coming up from below. But to make up for this there was the glorious scenery: cloud-piercing mountains and deep valleys, and near at hand tree-covered slopes, fantastic rocks, and everywhere masses of exquisite flowers. Here one could get away for an hour's quiet prayer alone, a thing that Isobel's soul had thirsted for in the crowded Chinese plain. "Physical hardship and spiritual luxury," Isobel called it.

They had a wonderful welcome from Leila Cooke,

naturally. When some of the Lisu Christians turned up, the Kuhns were not disappointed in them. These were splendid, sturdy, independent fellows, already missionaries among their own people, with whom it would be a privilege to work. And there was much to do, for these Lisu bird's-nest villages were scattered up and down the mountains and many of them had never yet been touched by the Gospel. Other trials and tests the Kuhns were to find out as the years went by, but none of the anxiety and suffering she had to bear made Isobel falter in her sureness that God had indeed called her to these dear people.

John became Big Brother immediately. While the two women were busy in the house—for Leila was to go to her husband as soon as the newcomers were settled— John looked out and saw some men at work in the vegetable garden. "I think I'll just go out and help those fellows," he exclaimed; his strong body was yearning for exercise. A few minutes later shouts and yells of laughter made Leila and Isobel run to see what the joke was. John was at the bottom of it, of course.

Two lads were hoeing a piece of rough ground to make a new garden; at least they should have been, but now they were rolling on the ground howling with laughter, while John was clowning with the hoe. He would solemnly raise it, give it a mighty whirl, and bring it down wallop! just missing the clod of earth he pretended to aim at. He could not yet speak their language, but he could show them that he knew how to share their fun. Laughter is the same all over the world!

Before Leila left she explained one of the serious troubles the Christian Lisu were undergoing.

"The chiefs get a lot of money selling opium, and they expect the villagers to grow the poppy to make it," she said. "The Christians know that opium smoking is a terrible thing—it makes men sick in mind and body, and the habit gets hold of them so that they cannot give it up, and will spend every penny they have to buy it; so the Christians refuse to plant it. The chiefs are persecuting them because of this, and my husband is having a hard struggle with the chiefs to get them to let the Christians alone. We don't know how it will end. Opium growing is forbidden by the Chinese Government, but this is such an out-of-the-way place that the chiefs do pretty much as they like. If a Government inspector does come here, he can probably be bribed not to report."

*   *   *

Then Leila went to join her husband, leaving the Kuhns with Moses, a Christian teacher, to interpret for them. They felt rather as if they had been thrown into the deep end of a swimming bath without knowing how to swim; but it made a good start, for they were absolutely forced to pick up the language as quickly as possible. Isobel especially soon became very good at it.

They came to love Moses. He was an unusually clever man, but so humble and modest that one had to know him well before one could realize what great gifts he had. He spoke Chinese, and had travelled right across China to Shanghai, where at once he had become a great favourite. The white people in Shanghai had given him a present of some fine white shirts, and the Cookes had been a little afraid that when he came back he might be vain and spoiled. But he had got straight into rough mountain clothes, and not a glimpse of those beautiful shirts had been seen by anyone. "We wonder what he did with them," Leila had said.

The mystery was solved when Moses conducted a baptismal service. Baptism among the Lisu was by dipping in a pool, just as John the Baptist baptized Jesus in Jordan. When he went into the pool Moses paused for a moment and rolled up his sleeves. As he did so the Kuhns saw for a moment the cuff of a white shirt under the blue homespun! Moses was wearing his friends' gift, but under his clothes, so that it would not show and make his poorer Lisu brethren envious.

Moses' wife was expecting a baby. It was an anxious time, for all her others had died at once. Isobel did her best though she had never been trained, and there was tremendous joy when a lovely, healthy baby girl was born. Moses was so glad and grateful, and so tender to the baby, that Isobel could only go on her knees and thank God. Then came a blow.

A messenger came from Allyn Cooke, six days away over the mountains. "Please ask Moses to come and help us here for three months. The work is growing—we need him."

"Oh," cried Isobel, "we *can't* ask Moses to go just now! Three months—he will miss all the first joy of his baby, the first smile, the first laugh. I can't tell him."

But she had to. When she gave Moses the message he gave a great start, then turned and looked up at the snowy mountain peaks. Peace came into his face, and he said quietly, "I will go if the Lord wants me to go."

Isobel prayed, "If the Lisu can produce such wonderful people as Moses, will You take my life and use it in teaching them?"

The Lord gave her many more like Moses.

7

UNDER THE SHADOW

THAT month among the Lisu was such a happy one that the Kuhns begged Mr. Fraser to let them move in as a family and remain to work there. Isobel so loved the place and the people that she was sure she could stand the hard life. Mr. Fraser wrote back that they might stay until their furlough, so at the end of 1934 a regular procession might have been seen winding its way over the mountains: Isobel and little Kathryn, now three years old, in a carrying chair, John riding Jasper, the wise but wilful old mule, and eleven pack horses bearing food stores, clothes and bedding, tools for building, oil for lighting, books, medicine—all they would need for that remote region where there were no shops, no doctors, and no post office nearer than a day's journey away.

There, in the House that John Built—though he was not a builder he made it so strong that it lasted for twenty years—they had hard times and happy times, and though the hard times were very bad it was the happy times that Isobel remembered best. There was the bad time when little Kathryn went down with fever, and it took a fortnight for the doctor's advice to reach them; there was the worse time when John was away pioneering, and Isobel fell ill, so ill that her Lisu friends, who had no idea what to do, thought she would surely die. But God had much work for her to do, and she recovered in the end.

Then came furlough, and a joyful year among friends and families, with much travelling about to meetings where they told about their work in China and among the Lisu. Isobel had a remarkable gift for telling her stories so vividly that her hearers seemed to know the actual people, and always she ended by asking for prayers, constant, steady prayers, for the Christians trying to live a new life among their heathen neighbours. Before the end of their furlough she had a number of faithful prayer friends whose intercession bore her up through the trial years to come.

Early in 1937 the Kuhns were all ready to sail for China, when news came that war between Japan and China, long expected, had broken out at last. All missionary sailings must be delayed.

"But why?" exclaimed Isobel. "The war is far away in the north. Yunnan, in the extreme south-west, is nowhere near the fighting. We shall be perfectly safe."

"Now, Belle dear, don't try to run the Mission," John began, but Isobel persisted.

"All obstacles are not from God. Let us put our case to Headquarters before we give in. Perhaps they are thinking about Kathryn's schooling, but there is no need for her to go to Chefoo, you know. There is the little school at Kunming, and she could stay with her aunt Kathryn there."

At Chefoo, on the east coast of China, there was a good school for missionaries' children, and as Kathryn was nearly seven it was necessary that she should have some education, and also little friends of her own age.

"Well," said John, "let us ask God to direct us. We haven't had our evening prayers yet."

He reached for his Bible, and opened it at the place marked for their evening reading.

"Belle, you win!" he exclaimed. "It is Psalm 91—'He that dwelleth in the secret place of the Most High shall abide under the shadow of the Almighty . . . Thou shalt not be afraid for the terror by night, nor for the arrow that flieth by day . . . For He shall give His angels charge concerning thee, to keep thee in all thy ways.' There is our answer!"

When they had prayed, he put the case to Headquarters, and it was agreed that missionaries to south China might safely sail.

But if Isobel had known what she was to go through in the next ten years, even her brave heart must have trembled.

*   *   *

When the boat arrived at Hong Kong, she was happily looking forward to meeting her Lisu friends again. Even having to part with Kathryn would not be too bad, for at Kunming, in the care of her aunt Mrs. Harrison (Kathryn Kuhn had married a missionary) she would be able to see her parents during the holidays, and letters, though they took a long time, could be regularly sent to and fro. The first shock came to her when the Kuhns found a telegram waiting for them: "Send Kathryn to Chefoo with Grace Liddell."

It looked as though Chefoo was not in danger, and of course it was a much bigger and better school than the small one at Kunming. But it meant parting from little daughter for at least two years, and with the country at war who could say how much longer they might be separated? Isobel thought her heart would break. How *could* she send Kathryn so far away, for such a long time? But it must be done, and she must not let the child be made unhappy. Miss Liddell, who was going to teach at Chefoo, was the kindest person possible, and little Kathryn loved and trusted her at once. It was all for the best—oh yes—God would take care of them, only the parting was agony. It was six years before mother and daughter met again.

Sitting in the train on the way to Kunming, the journey she thought she would have had with Kathryn beside her, Isobel prayed about her loss. In her heart her Lord answered her: "My dear, you must try to be a soldier. Don't *fondle* your grief. Think of something helpful. You will have many more partings to face, and you must learn to be brave about them."

"I will try, Lord," Isobel promised, and never again did she allow sorrow to break her heart.

Another disappointment waited for her. She and John were not to go back to the Lisu! Mr. Fraser wanted John as his assistant Superintendent in West Yunnan, and besides, after Isobel's serious illness before furlough, he still did not think her strong enough for the mountain work. They were to go to Paoshan.

This time Isobel did not rebel, though her heart was sad. She knew how well John, with his fine knowledge of the Chinese language, was fitted to assist Mr. Fraser. She would make the best of her share of the work. All the same, she was anxious about her Lisu friends, for the news that came out of Lisuland showed that they were having a difficult time. Most earnestly she prayed for them, and for herself, that she might follow God's guidance, *wherever it led*. And one day in her morning prayer the message came to her in the words of the prophet Zechariah: "At that time I will bring you again."

There were times when Isobel was not sure that a word of this sort was from God; she knew it might be only her own heart's wishes. But this time, somehow, she *knew*, and a great joy flooded her. She was going to be sent back to the work she loved best, and it would be in God's own way.

*   *   *

Sure enough, a little over a month after they arrived at Paoshan, a letter came from Mr. Fraser asking them to take a trip into Lisuland because the troubles there were getting worse. There might be a bad quarrel, and someone who knew the language well must go and settle things. He himself was too busy and too far away. It must be John and Isobel!

"Remember," Mr. Fraser's letter went on, "this is not permanent. You do not need to move all your things in, but you will need enough to set up housekeeping for a few months." A new Lisu missionary was to go with them and start learning the language.

Isobel was still sure that their stay would be longer than a few months. When they arrived they found that the heart of the trouble was a misunderstanding of the

Bible's teaching. What the leaders of the Church needed was some regular training in Bible study, and the best time for that would be during the rainy season, when work in the fields was impossible. So the Rainy Season Bible School was begun, and in later years became quite an adventure! The stay in Lisuland was lengthened in order to get it well going.

The Chinese-Japanese war went on, but Yunnan remained untouched, as the Kuhns had foreseen. Letters came from Kathryn, telling that she was happy and well at school. John and Isobel prepared to take a trip over the border to the tribes in Burma, when there came stunning news: Mr. Fraser was dead! He had fallen suddenly ill, and God took him to Himself.

With no one in charge, all missionaries just stayed where they were until a new Superintendent should be appointed. The Kuhns stayed in Lisuland! In 1939 war broke out in Europe, and the Japanese war went on, but America was not involved yet. When a new mission Superintendent was appointed for Yunnan, the province was divided into East and West, and John was made Assistant Superintendent of the West. That meant that he had to supervise the Chinese as well as the Lisu work, and Isobel had often to be left alone. They discussed whether they ought to move out to Paoshan, but Isobel felt strongly that she ought to remain with the Lisu, even if John must be away for months at a time.

The Lisu Christians understood how much they owed to Ma-ma (lady-teacher). "We would never have had Ma-pa (man-teacher) if Ma-ma had not loved us so dearly" one deacon was heard saying. Years before, Mr.

Fraser had asked for two men for the Lisu tribe, and had been rather disappointed when what he got was "only a girl". Before he died, he knew how much that "girl" was worth.

*   *   *

Isobel said afterwards that 1942 was for her "a horror of great darkness". The Japanese war had been going from bad to worse; province after province of China was overrun, until only the far west remained. Then, suddenly, they struck at the American Fleet in Pearl Harbor, America was in the war, and Americans, Canadians and British were all enemies of the Japanese. The Japanese swept over Malaya and into Burma, trying to cut the Burma Road, the only way now by which supplies could reach China from the west.

John was called to conference in Chungking, away to the north, the war-time capital of China. Isobel stayed with her Lisu, praying for John's safety, for the journey was a perilous one and almost every day Chungking was bombed by the Japanese.

Next, she had to bear the news that Chefoo had been captured, and all Americans and British interned—little Kathryn among them. No more regular letters, only an occasional little note smuggled out to tell her mother that she was alive and well.

Then there was Lucius. Lucius was the Kuhns' right-hand man at the Mission, a fine Lisu Christian on whom Isobel had grown to depend. He looked after her in travelling, guarded her, befriended her—and now he had to go too. It was for a happy reason; he married a charming

Christian girl, and set up house with her across the Salween river. Isobel rejoiced with him, but how she missed his understanding ways!

To cap it all, she developed a raging toothache—and the nearest qualified dentist was at Kunming! That would have meant a month's journey in the old days, but now the Burma Road was built it could be done in about a fortnight. That tooth must be seen to, so Isobel called porters to carry her things and take her out to Paoshan. In Kunming she could meet John on his way back from Chungking, and they could go back together.

It is difficult to see any blessing in a toothache, but Isobel was a little comforted to find that Lucius meant to go with her as far as Paoshan. He was building his new house, and Paoshan was the best place to buy nails, he said. So the first part of the journey was made quite happily with Lucius' cheerful companionship, and mercifully the pain in the tooth died down.

At Paoshan Isobel was faced with the Burma Road! She dreaded it. It was far worse than the old slow journey by chair or horseback or on foot, for the overloaded trucks, driven by reckless drivers, whirled and swayed along above sheer precipices, round hairpin bends, bouncing and clattering, and quite often a truck would miss the road and roll over and over to destruction. Travellers would pass those grim reminders of danger as they clung to their jolting seats (if they were lucky enough to have seats). Nevertheless for the first part of the way she was fortunate, for she got a lift in a private car driven by two American airmen.

Her Bible reading on the morning before they started

gave her another of God's messages. "And behold, I am with thee, and will keep thee in all places whither thou goest." That was said to Jacob, fleeing from his home and the anger of his brother, but, as Isobel said, "it sprang out of the page" and she knew it was for her. Lucius came in to tie up her bedding bundle, and she repeated the words to him in Lisu. He beamed, and went on—for he knew the passage well—" 'And will bring thee again into this land.' He's going to bring you back again!"

Isobel stared. Of course she was coming back! Later she was to understand that it was Lucius who had taken the real message. How nearly, but for God's guidance, she did not come back!

*　　*　　*

The American airmen were tough, but they were kind to her. All went well for the first four days; then the car broke down, miles from anywhere. The Americans could not speak Chinese.

"We'll just step into the road and persuade the next truck that comes along to give us a lift—with these!" They pulled out their guns.

"Oh, don't do that!" begged Isobel. "I can speak Chinese. I'll interpret for you."

In the end she did not have to, for a white man appeared in a jeep and offered to take them on. He had no room for all their baggage, so they had to leave it locked up in the abandoned car.

"We'll come back and fetch it later," promised the airmen cheerfully, forgetting they were not now in America. Of course when they did come back everything had been stolen, so Isobel lost her bedding roll and all her spare clothes. It was a foretaste of misfortunes to follow.

She was beginning to feel very ill from her poisoned tooth, but the thought of the warm welcome she would get from her sister-in-law Kathryn and her husband cheered her up as she made her way to the well-known house. She pushed open the garden gate, expecting to hear a shout of welcome when someone saw her. But there was no call. She went into the house. It was silent and empty! "Kay" and David must be away—and she was feeling more and more ill. What should she do?

Then there was a patter of small feet and a little rosy Chinese maiden came running. It was Eva, daughter of a Chinese pastor, who lived with the family and helped in the house, in order to get more education. She was a tiny little thing who looked like a child, but was really twenty-one and most capable. She and Isobel knew each other well.

"Oh, Yang-si-muh" (Isobel's Chinese name), "the Harrison family are all away in the country for some meetings! But come in—I will take care of you."

Isobel needed care. The tooth had stopped aching, but the poison was seeping all through her body, and she was seriously ill. John was wired for to come to her at once. It was some days before the doctors found out what was the matter, and got the tooth pulled out. The dentist said that one day more and her life could not have been saved!

In those days when she lay in bed, growing weaker and weaker, Isobel learned to know Eva as never before. The girl was a little jewel. She was a "full-time" Christian, who did everything, whether it was studying, or cooking, or cleaning, or marketing, or, as now, caring for a sick friend, as well as she could possibly do it. She was brave, too, as Isobel was to find. They became close friends, and remained so for many years.

*   *   *

John arrived from Chungking, the Harrisons came back from the country; the war news grew worse and worse. The Japanese were advancing through Burma, the British and Americans retreating. John heard that Lashio, a town he had thought of visiting on the way back from Chungking, had been taken. If the doctors had not wired him about Isobel's illness, he must have been captured. Kunming had air raid alarms. John, as Superintendent, felt that he must go west to warn missionary families that they must leave at once.

The awful day came when Isobel heard that Paoshan had been bombed, suddenly and without warning, on a market day at noon. Now all Yunnan was in a panic, and refugees crowded on the Burma Road to reach Kunming. And where was John? Isobel wondered. Could he have been in Paoshan when it was bombed?

John came back, safe and sound, with a group of missionaries and the Harrisons' little boy, who had been at school at Tali. They had had some terrifying adventures, but all were safe. Then off went John again to try to get other workers out.

Rumours came thick and fast. The Japanese were pushing up the rivers from Burma—would they get into Lisuland? Others were said to be approaching from the east. The British consul advised the missionaries to move out, going either northwards, or by air to India.

"But my husband has not come back!" Isobel protested. "How can I leave when I don't know where he is?" Though she had prayed, she got no guidance. She decided that this meant she was to stay where she was.

Things grew more desperate. Finally the consul *ordered* them to leave with the next convoy; all her friends were leaving, and Isobel consented, much against her will, to go. They could take with them only a bedding roll and one suitcase. What, of all their possessions, should they choose to go in that suitcase? And they would have to leave dear Eva, for she was Chinese. Tears streamed down her face as she helped her friends to pack.

"If only we could take her with us!" said Kay perplexedly. "But it is hard enough to make room for British women."

Eva went with them to the convoy to say a last good-bye—and the miracle happened. The R.A.F. captain saw the little Chinese girl sobbing bitterly, and asked what she was crying for.

"She wants to come with us," answered Mr. Harrison, without hope. "She doesn't want to be left behind."

"Oh, well, she's not very big," said the kindly captain. "Let her get in. That's O.K."

So, without spare clothes, bedding or any preparation, Eva was bundled into the truck, and the convoy started—north-eastward, not west, into central China. Day after day, huddled in the back of the truck, with a typewriter and a spare tyre under her and boxes of ammunition under those, Isobel had plenty of time to think. Every day was taking her farther from John and the Lisu; her companion, Evelyn Gibson, had left her fiancé in Yunnan, and often Isobel heard the poor girl softly crying. Kay, with her little son and Eva, was in another truck.

"Am I doing right?" Isobel wondered. "God has not told me clearly to come this way. Ought I to have refused to go? Am I out of God's will?"

Then as she prayed she remembered her message: "Behold, I am with thee, and will keep thee in *all places* whither thou goest, and will *bring thee again* into this land."

"O Lord," she prayed, "I know You will keep Your promises. Maybe I was wrong to let myself be pushed into this, but You didn't stop me, so I know that *some time* You will bring me back to my people."

     ★   ★   ★

The convoy was making for Chengtu, the capital of Szechwan Province in West China. Many missionaries from many societies had gathered there, also schools and colleges which had had to move from their own towns, and the place was full up with refugees. Before they reached Chengtu a telegram was handed to Isobel and her party, saying that there was no room for them; they must get off the convoy at Lusien and stay with a Mr. and Mrs. Lea.

"Has Yunnan fallen to the Japanese?" was the first question Isobel asked her hosts. They had had no certain news all the time they were travelling.

"Why, no," said Mr. Lea, much surprised. "In fact the news has been quite good lately. The Japanese have been chased back over the Salween river and held there."

So their flight had been perfectly useless! John was lost, Kathryn was interned, she was far from home—and even if she could find a way to get back she had not enough money to pay for the journey. There was one comfort; the Leas had had word that the children captured by the Japanese were being kindly treated.

"The best thing you can do," advised Mr. Lea, "is to settle down here for the time and help with the Church work."

It was good advice, and Isobel took it. It was not work she liked, and she had to learn a new dialect of Chinese. She had to face again the dirt and lice of the Chinese homes she visited. All the time her heart ached with longing for her own people, the Lisu, for her little daughter, for her loved husband and companion.

"O Lord," she wailed, "I'm only human! I want someone of my own! Why must everything be taken from me?"

It almost made things worse when a letter came through from John. He was safe and well. There were great opportunities—and no missionaries! Nearly all had fled. "What ought I to do? Oh, what ought I to do?" wondered Isobel.

8

"I WILL BRING THEE AGAIN"

ISOBEL hung on to that promise. She wrote to the Director of the Mission, telling him of the opportunities her husband wrote about, and saying that she felt she ought to return. When at last the answer came, she was told that she ought to stay where she was until her husband invited her to return. That was enough for Isobel—had not John said how much he wished she were with him? But how should she manage about money? Would she be able to get transport? Very few trucks were going south in those days. Could she, a woman, travel all that way alone? Above all, what was God's will?

She went out to a Chinese cemetery, where she knew she would be alone, and there among the graves she poured out her heart.

"If I am to go, Lord," she said, "there are four things I need: money for the fares; a letter from John definitely asking me to come back, to show to the Director; trucks going to Yunnan to take me there; and a companion. If You wish me to go, please supply these needs."

In just over a day her prayer was answered fully. Letters arrived from America with a special gift of money; John sent a telegram, urging her to come to him; Mr. Lea found a convoy of three trucks going back to Kunming; and Eva asked if she might come too!

The money gift was the most wonderful. When they were on furlough, John had used part of a legacy from his father to help a young Bible student finish her course. She had promised to pay it back, but the Kuhns had just laughed at that and forgotten it. Now, by the same mail, arrived two letters written six months apart, each containing half the money—10,000 dollars altogether!

Eva was another miracle. She was Kathryn's friend and helper, and she had made herself so useful that Isobel would never have dared to ask for her. But finding Eva crying quietly over her sewing, Kay of course asked what was the matter, and found that the girl was longing to go back with Isobel.

"Eva says she wants to go and work with the Lisu. I haven't the money to pay her expenses back to Yunnan, but if you have enough to pay for her too, why, take her!"

"But, Kay, can you really do without her? She is such a jewel of a worker——"

"No, no, Isobel, if you want Eva, take her."

Isobel could have wished for nothing better.

*　　*　　*

Everything promised well on the day they started. The truck they were to ride in was a new one, and by paying extra they could have seats in the cab by the driver. That meant they would not have to perch outside on top of the baggage, exposed to rain and wind.

"These trucks are going right through to Kunming," said the manager of the company, bowing politely. "They are not allowed to pick up *yellow fish.*"

"Yellow fish" was the name for travellers whom the

drivers picked up by the way, putting the money for their fares into their own pockets instead of the firms'.

However, the manager might promise, but once away there was nothing to stop the drivers from doing as they pleased. All the way along they picked up "yellow fish". At the main cities they passed through, the company had inspection posts, but of course the "yellow fish" got off before they arrived and met them again on the other side of the town. This made the trucks unpleasantly crowded, but at first, with their seats in the cab, and staying overnight with missionary friends in the places they stopped at, Isobel and Eva were quite well treated. But when they came to the lonely mountain ranges into Yunnan, the driver dropped his pretences and became really rude and threatening.

One day he took on board some friends of his own, and wanted the seats in the cab for them.

"You are to get into the second truck," he said roughly to Isobel. "There's no room for your companion—she can ride in the back of my truck."

Let little Eva ride among those unpleasant passengers, all by herself? Not if Isobel knew it! Politely but firmly she said, "We can't be separated. We have paid for our seats. You have been taking on 'yellow fish', and if you don't give us our seats I'll report you to the company."

It was not a wise thing to say, for they were far from friends and quite at the man's mercy. He poured out a torrent of evil-sounding Chinese so fast that Isobel could not understand what he was saying, and Eva began to cry.

"Oh, Yang-si-muh," she sobbed. "I don't mind standing in the back of the truck! Don't make any fuss! He says he is going to throw us out on the mountainside and leave us to the wild beasts!"

It looked hopeless. No one in Kunming knew that they were coming, so no one would ask questions if they did not arrive. There was no one near to protect them—yes, but there was!

"Oh Lord, You promised——"

Before the prayer was completed a hand pulled at Isobel's sleeve, and a Chinese voice whispered, "Get into my cab, quick! Both of you!" It was the driver of the second truck. They sprang in and were whirled away, leaving the driver of the first truck swearing in the road.

"Lady, never do that again!" said their helper. "Next time you travel the Burma Road, you travel 'yellow fish'!"

★   ★   ★

Isobel hoped she never *would* have to travel that way again! But the driver proved a real friend. His was an old truck, and several times it had broken down on the road; but now it kept steadily on, well ahead of the others. The kindly driver took them right up to the Harrisons' house in Kunming, where Isobel's brother-in-law, David Harrison, gave them a hearty welcome.

Naturally Isobel wanted to push on to the west and join John, who was then at Tali. But David asked her if she would stay for a fortnight and teach his Bible classes, as he wanted to take a trip into the country to visit some Churches which needed his advice. Much as she hungered for her husband, Isobel agreed to this readily. The delay turned out to be useful; by the time David came back, a Friends' Ambulance Unit was going west, and they offered to take Isobel—and Eva too. For Eva was to get her wish and work with the Kuhns among the Lisu. What a relief that they had not to drive on that stretch of the Burma Road in a Chinese truck! They might not have been so lucky in finding a helpful driver!

A smooth run to Tali with the pleasant companions of the Friends' Ambulance Unit—then another shock. John was not there. He had gone on to Paoshan with Dr. Mei, the Chinese doctor, and his Medical Unit, to help the people who had been bombed on that dreadful day. Isobel could have wept.

"Shall I ever have anyone of my own to love me?" was her first thought. Then God's whisper came, "You must learn not to *lean* on earthly love. People are only human and they are bound to leave you at some time. Lean on Me. I will never let you down."

That was the lesson Isobel had been learning in those lonely, anxious months. From now on she was watchful to see that she did not depend too much even on the best and dearest.

For all that, it was clearly her duty to join John as soon as possible, so that she could go on with her work. Only how was it to be done? For all west of Tali was now a military zone. The Japanese were still on the west bank of the Salween river, right on the edge of Lisuland, and the Chinese army would not let anyone, not even American soldiers, go through. John had only been allowed in because he was with a Chinese Medical Unit! How would it be possible for a foreign woman to get the necessary pass?

She determined to go to Headquarters, to General Song, the General in command. She hated to do so. For one thing, she was so shabby. Her best clothes had been left in Paoshan, and they had been stolen in the looting which followed the bombing. Other clothes were lost when the car broke down on the way out. Missionary friends had given her some things, but they had not much to spare.

At the outer gate of General Song's estate the sentry looked contemptuously at the thin, pale, down-at-heels woman missionary. She was kept waiting for hours, and then sent home without a pass. She learned afterwards that they had not even troubled to give her application to General Song.

"Oh Lord," prayed Isobel, "I leave it to You."

And that very evening an officer arrived at the Mission house "to inform Mrs. Kuhn that General Song had telephoned to Paoshan and requested that John Kuhn come to Tali—the General providing transportation."

*　　　*　　　*

A few days later Isobel was in John's arms. "But what does it all mean?" she asked when the first greetings were over.

"No doubt the General wants us to do something for him!" grinned John. "We are to go to see him this afternoon, and then we shall know."

A very different reception they got at General Song's gate! Officials bowed to them politely and took them straight to the beautiful house where the General and his charming wife lived. The lady spoke very good English, though of course as both the Kuhns spoke Chinese it was not necessary to interpret. The General greeted them warmly and explained frankly what he wanted. John was quite right; he did want them to do something for him.

"The position is this," stated the General. "Our army checked the Japanese at the bridge over the Salween, as you know. But the enemy made their way north up the river to find another crossing, and the heathen tribes there received them and helped them. As soon as I got news of this I determined to send someone to explain to these poor people how dangerous it is to help the Japanese, and to make friends with them."

John and Isobel were each thinking the same thing: "Yes, that's all very well, but for hundreds of years you Chinese have neglected and despised the poor mountain tribes. Now you suddenly see that they have their uses!"

"I had to find someone who could speak their language," the General went on, "and naturally I thought of the tribal chiefs. I went into Lisuland to talk to them—and what did I find? They are all rotten with opium. They care for nothing but opium. They are no use at all. Then I remembered the good missionaries—yourself and your wife—such highly respected people—who know the Lisu well and can speak their language; so I sent for you. Will you help us to gain the friendship of the Lisu?"

"That is exactly what we have been doing all these years," answered John. "When war broke out we told them that if the Japanese came into their land they would oppose the Lisu being Christians, and that was enough for them. Have you noticed, sir, that on part of the west bank of the river where Lisu Christians live, the Japanese were turned back and have never got any further? But of course if you will send us back to Lisuland we shall be only too glad to explain matters to the heathen."

"I will give you a military escort right to your home, which I understand is at Oak Flat Village," the General promised. "And I appoint you adviser to the colonel in charge of the district."

A delicious feast at the Song mansion (when Chinese food is good it is *very* good!); a brand-new truck with a soldier escort; and then they were on their way west. Not without adventures; a very nasty accident on a precipitous road resulted in some of the soldiers being injured. At Paoshan horses were provided for the long trek into the mountains, and at last they were at home. The promise had been fulfilled, and the Lord had brought them again into this land.

9

BUSINESS AS USUAL

"MA-MA, strange soldiers! Just beyond Cow's Hump Village! Can they be Japanese?"

It was a Saturday morning. John was away, and Isobel was holding a Bible School for the young men, but as it was the week-end the students were all scattered in the surrounding villages, preaching or holding services. What should be done? If the Japanese were so near, ought they not to break up the Bible School and get away while there was time? Three white missionaries were staying with Isobel, and they held a council.

"Well," said Isobel firmly, "last time I ran away without waiting for God's clear word, I got into all sorts of trouble. As far as I am concerned I am going to remain until He tells me to go! Besides, the word I had in my Bible reading today was, 'Lord, Thou wilt ordain peace for us.' "

So it was agreed that they would carry on as usual, until they were sure if the strange soldiers were Japanese or not.

Next day, Sunday, was a bright, sunny day. No further news of the soldiers. Isobel wondered if the near-by villagers would come as usual to Oak Flat for the services; perhaps with these frightening rumours about they would not dare? But by midday several hundred had gathered, all rather nervous and asking what Ma-ma was going to do?

It reassured them to learn that Ma-ma was not going to run away, and that the Bible School would go on as usual. "I expect all the students to be back by nine o'clock on Monday morning for classes," she told the Lisu, and when they went back to their villages in the evening they spread the word that Ma-ma was not afraid. Everything would be all right.

Sure enough, all the students turned up in good time. Some of them had gone north in the direction of Cow's Hump Village, and they brought good news. The soldiers were not Japanese, but Chinese from another province, who wore a different uniform and spoke with a different accent. How glad was Isobel that she had decided to "wait on the Lord"!

*   *   *

Christmas, 1942, was a happy time, with hundreds of Lisu gathering at Oak Flat for the festival. Isobel asked the assembly how many young women and girls would be coming to the Girls' Bible School, held every year in February. There was no answer. The girls looked at one another and shook their heads doubtfully. Things were so unsettled; taxes were high—they might not be able to afford to come. Even the wives of the evangelists, whose board for the time of the School was paid by the Church, would not promise. They "hoped they would come". That was the best answer Isobel could get.

At the New Year, 1943, everything seemed quiet. The Chinese armies were holding the enemy in the west.

Should the missionaries prepare for the Girls' Bible School, even though they had no promises of attendance?

There were only two of them just then at Oak Flat, Charles Peterson and Isobel. John was away again, trying to rescue a missionary couple who had been caught behind the Japanese lines. He was often away in those days, and Isobel had learned to bear the separations with courage. This business of preparation was a serious one, for the dormitories where the girls slept were badly in need of repair, and new beds were needed. To get them fitted up would cost a good deal of the Mission's scanty money.

"Business as usual!" laughed Isobel. "If the Lord does not mean us to hold the school, He will stop us in time." So the practical repairs started, and besides that Isobel began to choose the new hymns which the girls would learn and take back to their villages. That was a part of the work which Isobel specially loved. She was very fond of music, and the Lisu had lovely voices and could sing in parts. A trained Lisu choir was something to listen to.

"Doesn't look much like the Bible School!" sighed Charles as the time drew near, for the weather had turned really bad. Snow on the mountains and an icy wind, drenching rain on the lower slopes. The girls who lived across the river had twenty miles of rough road to travel on their bare feet, and there was always the fear that even if they got to Oak Flat the river might rise while they were there, so that they would not be able to get away again. If they were caught in a snowstorm they might die of exposure.

On the Saturday before the School was to start, about a dozen girls from the near side of the river gathered.

Sunday was stormy. But on Monday the rain let up, though the skies were sullen and grey. Would any more girls come? Isobel started the School with the girls already there, scarcely hoping for any more.

At sunset came a ringing shout: "Girls from the west bank are coming!" Out they all ran—or tottered rather, for the ground was deep in slippery mud—and there they saw them coming along the mountain trail, their books and bedding slung over their shoulders in big bags, or carried mountain fashion on their backs with a strap round the forehead. Behind them their brothers and husbands followed, loaded with the grain that was to be their food.

"We were afraid you wouldn't come——"

"Come into the kitchen and get warm——"

"How lovely to see you——"

"Oh, *what* a time we had getting here——"

Such chatter and laughter as they gathered in the warm kitchen, ate a hot supper and told of their adventures; and when all met for evening prayers Isobel counted thirty-three students. And that Monday was the only decently dry day for a week!

★   ★   ★

Girls' Bible School over, and most successfully—what next? A new venture for Isobel, Charles and Eva; a school for young boys from ten years upwards. Most of these lads were cowherds. Their duty was to watch the cattle all day and every day, lest they stray, or get to fighting and push one another down the rocky mountain slopes. But in March, before the spring ploughing, other members of the family would be able to look after the cattle and set the boys free for Bible School. March it had to be; and March brought more alarms.

Rumours came that the Japanese were on the move again. Soldiers were posted at the ferries, ready to destroy them if the enemy should try to cross. Suppose boys from the west bank came to the School, and then were not able to get home? The weather was bad, and the cook gave notice. Isobel went on with her preparations.

Thirty-seven boys turned up! In spite of war-planes overhead and sometimes a dog-fight in the air, the boys enjoyed the school so much that when they got home they had such a lot to tell that nobody could get a word in edgeways. Their families gathered to listen to their stories; so the Gospel spread and the Lisu Church was strengthened.

August of that year brought a great joy to Isobel and John; a little boy was born to them, red-haired Daniel Kreadman Kuhn. The baby brought more worries, of course—it was not easy to get milk for him and Isobel now had her little one as well as her other cares. What she would have done without dear Eva she could not imagine. The Chinese girl installed herself as nurse, and if Danny cried at night, Eva was up in a flash to attend to him so that Isobel could get her much-needed sleep.

John was called away to a conference at Chungking, and the very next day Charles Peterson came down with rheumatic fever. At the same time the boy who looked after the goats, from which Danny got his milk, fell ill, and so did the girl who did the laundry. And it rained.

Charles's cabin was further down the mountain than

the Kuhns', so all his meals had to be carried down a slope slippery and treacherous with mud. He was in horrible pain, bravely borne, and in addition to her other cares Isobel was troubled that he could not have the skilled nursing he needed. And the Rainy Season Bible School was due to start in November! Could it possibly be carried through without Charles's help?

"Send to Luda for Orville Carlson. He's good at the language, and if they could spare him I'm sure he'd come," suggested Charles weakly.

"All right," agreed Isobel a trifle grimly. She had half wondered if it would not be a relief to cancel the Bible School for this once; but—"business as usual."

A messenger was sent off to Luda, and in due time Orville Carlson did arrive. But in the meantime there were dark days for the Mission at Oak Flat.

        ★   ★   ★

One evening in particular Isobel never forgot, though she made a funny story of it when all was over. It was a Sunday. Eva had gone to church, while Isobel was to go to bed early and get some rest. However, she felt she ought to go down to Charles's cabin before she turned in, and see how he was getting on. She found him in agony, so bad that he needed a shot of morphine to dull the pain. Isobel had never given an injection; John had always done that. Carefully she sterilized the needle, and that was not an easy job over a half-dead coal fire.

"Charles, I don't really know how to do it," she faltered. "I'm afraid I shall hurt you."

"Oh, it's easy," said Charles, taking the syringe. "Like

this." He pressed the plunger, and shot the carefully sterilized needle straight through the window!

It was the only one they had, so Isobel had to go out with a lantern into the dark and wet, hunt in the mud, and then take the precious needle up the mountainside to her house and sterilize it all over again. Small troubles? Yes—but to an exhausted woman, with a desperately suffering patient, on a dark stormy night, it seemed just about the last straw. All the same, it became a kind of family joke: "Oh, it's easy. All you do is—shoot it out of the window!"

So the months went by. All the Bible Schools were held, and all were blessed. The year 1943 came to an end. In 1944 the Japanese withdrew. Wonderful news came of little Kathryn.

The Japanese had agreed to free some of the interned children, a special ship had been sent from America, and the Kuhns' daughter had sailed safely home. Furlough was due in the autumn. They would all be together as a family again!

As Isobel sat in the rattling truck that was taking them on the first stage of the journey, with John beside her and baby Danny on her knee, her heart was filled with thanksgiving. Dangers—harassments—anxiety for friends and loved ones—weariness and loneliness—through it all "business as usual", the Father's business, had been carried on.

10

DANGER ON ALL SIDES

A WONDERFULLY happy furlough, in a little home of their own; Kathryn going daily to school nearby; John taking a refresher course at a college; a fenced garden for Danny to play in; the companionship of like-minded people—all this gave the Kuhns refreshment and strength for the ordeals that waited for them. Isobel revelled in a peaceful, normal home-life, such as she had not had since her marriage.

She knew very well that it could not last. She was a soldier on duty, and when called back to the front line she must go. Actually it was John who went first. The war ended, and missionary superintendents were asked to go back; but the war-torn land was not yet safe for women and children. So John left for Yunnan a year before Isobel and Danny could follow him. The parting was hard, but Isobel was glad to have the extra year with Kathryn, now a tall girl of fourteen. She, of course, would have to stay with friends in America and go on with her schooling.

In 1947 the summons came.

★   ★   ★

"Mummy! My horse has bells and yours hasn't!" three-year-old Danny shouted in triumph from his high perch. Two careful Lisu walked by his side to see that he did not fall off. "My horse rides bumpily," Danny added.

They were climbing the familiar trail into Lisuland, Isobel and Danny and a train of porters. John had been left behind for the time in Paoshan, attending to Mission business, but Isobel could not wait to get back and see how her Lisu friends were faring. To Danny it was all a magnificent adventure.

Already a shadow was falling on Isobel's heart. She had noticed that the little villages where they used to stay by the road were all deserted. "Too many robbers about!" her porters had told her. As they at last came in sight of her own home on the mountain side, she was taken aback to see how dilapidated it looked. The walls sagged dangerously towards the precipice, the thatch had blown off in patches, inside everything was dusty. The caretakers had done a bit of sweeping, but plainly they had been lazy.

It was not long before other disappointments showed themselves; the hardest disappointments a missionary has to bear—backsliding. Many whom Isobel had thought well-rooted Christians had grown cold. Still professing Christianity, they had become greedy, sly and hypocritical. There were divisions and quarrelling. A deacon had to be put out of office, and in revenge he persecuted the Kuhns in all sorts of petty ways. And there were the robbers who lurked in the caves of the mountains; disbanded soldiers who were too lazy and shiftless to get honest work, most of them. One dreadful night Isobel could hear them prowling round the house, and she lay there shaking. She trusted in God, but He *did* allow missionaries to be killed! Was this the time? John was away, as he so often had to be.

No; men from the village had seen the robbers, and drove them away. Lucius, that staunch and splendid Lisu Christian who lived with his sweet wife Mary at Village of Olives across the river, urged her to leave Oak Flat and come to live with him. But as yet Isobel did not think it right to leave.

It was after John returned that a really terrible quarrel blew up, caused by the resentful ex-deacon, Keh-deh-seh-pa. It was clear to John that, being obliged so often to go away, he could not possibly leave his wife and child in Oak Flat. Isobel grieved bitterly at having to abandon her large house, dilapidated though it was, and go and live in the middle of a noisy village further down the valley; and she sorrowed over the feeling of defeat that drove her from the place where she had seen so many souls renewed in Christ. But God was guiding them, as she presently understood.

At the end of 1948 they moved to the small house Lucius had built for them near his own big one. Four months later Oak Flat was invaded by a band of robbers who called themselves Communists; Keh-deh-seh-pa joined with them—and what would have happened to Isobel and Danny if they had remained in the village can easily be imagined! She found, too, that at Olives she could reach heathen Lisu who had never before heard the Gospel; so she acknowledged that, as always, God knew best.

★   ★   ★

Communists! That was a danger which the Kuhns had not foreseen, and presently it became clear that all missionary work in Yunnan was threatened. Some so-called Communists were simply brigands, whom the Communists permitted to stir up trouble, and then cast off when the Red Army took control. Others really did mean to bring a better way of life to China, only they thought they could do it by force, and left God out of account. While Isobel and the Lisu Christians tried to carry on their daily work of teaching and preaching, hold-ing the regular Bible Schools and building up the Church, the Communist armies were rapidly spreading over China, driving the "Nationalist" forces before them; and with the regular Communists were the Lo-zi-lo-pa, brutal brigands of the worst kind.

It was at Christmas time that news arrived that the Lo-zi-lo-pa were making for Village of Olives, to fight with the young chief, Dwan. He was nearly as great a villain as the brigands; whether he would be able to defend the village or not, it seemed certain that there would be battle—and horrible danger for Isobel and Danny. John was expected home, but he did not come.

The conviction was pressed on Isobel that the time had come for her to get Danny away. He was six years old, he needed education, and all this evil and turmoil about him was not good for a small boy. His mother had learned her lesson, however—*do not be in a hurry*; wait until the Lord shows the way. They would have to get out through Burma, for the way eastward was closed by fighting; and she wanted to see John before she left.

Day after day went by, and no attack came! Instead,

news that Chief Dwan had made peace with the Communists and submitted to them. The danger had passed for the time, for the Lo-zi-lo-pa would not be turned loose on Olives to wreak vengeance on the chief. At last John turned up; he had been delayed by fighting on the Burma Road. He had brought with him hundreds of tracts in the Lisu language, and he had brought Eva! She had begged to come with them when they met in Tali on their return, but John and Isobel insisted that she should finish her nurse's training.

"John, I have been thinking that I must get Danny out of this."

John, with a sad face, agreed. "Yes. The Communists distrust all foreigners and they don't believe in God. They are bound to hinder our work, if not stop it entirely. You should get out soon, before they take complete control."

"They are not all bad," said Isobel thoughtfully. "There was a girl soldier who came with the Communist party which visited us after the truce; I had a talk with her, and she admitted that we had done wonderful work among the Lisu. She said she could see the difference between the Christian and the heathen Lisu. 'The heathen are opium sots, liars, thieves and you cannot depend on them. The Christians,' she said, 'are like us.' "

"They think they can change men's hearts without God's help. They will find out their mistake in time," sighed John. "Meanwhile, I fear that we shall not for long be allowed to work in peace. But you are quite right, dear, you must get Danny away, and perhaps you will be allowed to come back to me."

"You won't come too?" Isobel had expected this, but it was hard.

"I must stay as long as I can. Look, Belle, let us do one last thing together before we part. Let's hold the biggest Bible School ever! I've got all this literature for the students to take away with them, and if we have to go everything will depend on these Lisu Christians. They must be well prepared."

That Bible School was the best Isobel had known. When the students went out preaching at week-ends there were many conversions, and the literature "sold like hot cakes" as Isobel put it. Nurse Eva was a blessing, as usual—she treated the sick, and all by herself did operations on diseased eyes that made her fame spread far and wide among the mountains. It was a glad and encouraging memory for Isobel to carry away with her. She never saw Eva again, but heard later that the brave girl, in Communist China, was studying to be a doctor.

As she and Danny and their porters set out, on a threatening February day, for the perilous snowy pass into Burma, Isobel felt in her heart that she would never go back to the Lisu. She was both right and wrong.

*　　　*　　　*

Three days later they were approaching the pass, when the rain came. That meant that above them the pass itself would be blocked by snow. All that day, all night and all next day it rained. The porters, Christian Lisu who did not want to lose their beloved Ma-ma, looked serious.

"We can't possibly get over the pass," they said. "We must go back to Olives."

Isobel prayed: "Lord, if this obstacle is from Thee, I accept it. If not, I refuse it!" To the porters she said, "If tomorrow we turn back, and then the sun comes out, wouldn't you feel foolish?' Let us leave it this way: if tomorrow it is not raining, we will take it as a sign that we are to go on. And if, when we reach the snow line, we find that the track is covered, we will even then turn back. I don't want to risk your lives. But I have found that if we go as far as we can, God often opens up the rest of the way. Will you do it?"

If they had not been Christians, they would have refused. But they had faith, and they agreed. Next day, though cloudy and threatening, it did not actually rain, and they started up.

The clouds hung low over the mountains, and soon they were travelling in cold wet fog. The Lisu, usually such merry comrades on the road, plodded in silence. Isobel was riding, Danny carried in a chair. Sometimes they could hardly see each other through the mist. Isobel wondered and prayed. Was she doing right? Would they ever be able to find the trail when they reached the snow? Then out of the gloom two dark figures emerged— a couple of Lisu coming back from a trading expedition in Burma. At least they had got safely over!

"How's the top?" the porters called.

"The snow is deep, but there's a large party of us, and we have trampled it down pretty thoroughly. If you hurry up you should find the way by our footprints. My, didn't we have a time getting over!"

They laughed and sprang away down the steep path. Presently Isobel's party met another group of the traders, and again asked how things were.

"It's beginning to snow again, but you can make it," was the answer. "Follow our footprints!"

It was now midday, and all were hungry, but they did not dare to stop and cook food. Isobel shared a slice of bread and a bit of cheese with Danny, and on they went, and always up. The pass at last! Here the snow was deep, the trail wound to and fro before beginning to descend. Without those deeply trampled footprints they never could have found the way. Even so it was desperate going. Once Isobel's mule sank in the snow and had to be hauled out by two men. Those who were carrying Danny's chair had to take him on their backs, as the way was too slippery for them to manage the poles. Young Danny, in his rain-coat and rubber hat, was the best off of them all, and he cheered the way considerably by singing at the top of his voice; but Isobel was soaked to the waist. At last they were over the pass.

*   *   *

That deliverance helped Isobel's faith in the long, difficult journey back to America. Through the Burmese jungle to the town of Myitkyina; from Myitkyina to Rangoon, from Rangoon to Bangkok, Bangkok to Hong Kong, then a ship to America—again and again Isobel was at her wits' end, over money, over visas, over transport; but always, every time, came help at the moment it was most needed. Home at last, and Kathryn, a grown-up Kathryn, now a college student, old enough to be a dear friend and companion to her mother as well as a loved daughter.

A year later, John came home. He had had a wonderful and unexpected year of freedom to work, until a change in the Communist policy pushed all missionaries out of China.

And that seemed to be the end of the Kuhns' missionary life.

11

"BUT WE ARE OLD . . ."

ALL missionaries had to leave China, and the China Inland Mission had worked only in that land. Was that to be the end of the C.I.M.?

In the countries that border China (Malaya, Burma, Thailand) many Chinese are living, and in the mountains between live tribes like the Karens, Miao, Lisu, in villages to many of which no Christian messenger has ever come. So the Overseas Missionary Fellowship of the China Inland Mission was formed; the O.M.F. for short. Experienced missionaries who knew the Chinese language would be needed, and just such missionaries were the Kuhns. John was asked to go to Thailand as O.M.F. Superintendent.

Isobel's heart sank. Leave the little home she had made so pretty, leave young Kathryn just beginning life, and little Danny the schoolboy, and all her kind friends?

"But, John, we are old!" she protested (she was only fifty!). "It is a young man's job, a pioneering job. We should have to learn a new language—Thai; and all that mountain climbing——"

"Listen, Belle," said steady John. "We can use the Chinese language with almost all the mountain tribes; they need us badly—there are tribes that have never yet been reached, and if we don't go *now* the door may close. Among them are some of our own Lisu tribespeople. And you needn't do any rough climbing if you don't feel up to it. They have appointed me Superintendent, and your job will be to make a home for missionaries passing to and fro, and to welcome and 'mother' young missionaries when they come out. You can do it."

Isobel knew she could—she ought—she would.

    *   *   *

Base Camp; Advance Camp; Summit Camp. That was how Isobel described the new work in Thailand. Her work lay at Base Camp—Chiengmai, in North Thailand, at the end of the railway, with banks, post, telegraph. Advance Camps were the next stage forward among the mountains, where the tribes could be met with and contacts made: and Summit Camps were the distant, untouched villages.

Life in Chiengmai was very different from the solitary work at Oak Flat or Olives, and Isobel feared that she would be swamped with activities. Missionaries of many societies had stations in Chiengmai. There was great friendliness, and much entertaining of guests, generally unexpected ones. It certainly was not dull. As O.M.F. missionaries came and went, they brought stories of their adventures and discoveries, all of which Isobel collected and later made into a book. She had already written, in her bright and moving style, several books about her work and that of other missionaries of the China Inland Mission.

She might think she was old, but once back on the

mission field the pioneering call was too strong, and whenever she could she went with John on his journeys as Superintendent.

"Now, Belle," John had said firmly, "remember, this time you are not going to the Lisu, you are going to help me. In China we often had to be separated, but in Thailand we are going to stick together."

So when John told her that they were to take a trip of two hundred miles into the land of the Miao, she agreed cheerfully—though she would much rather have gone in search of the Lisu. As it turned out, that was just what she did. Before they started John changed his mind. Someone was needed to go to a Lisu village, and Isobel was the only one who spoke the language. She and a young language student, Edna McLaren, were to go.

So it was that Isobel found herself, just before dawn a day or two later, lying on a bamboo platform looking eastwards over the dark mass of tumbled mountains. As the sun rose red through the grey night mists the sharp ridges took shape, she could see the little shanties of the Lisu with the smoke of early morning fires curling up. By her side lay Edna, wrapped in her blanket, and a little way off, only separated by a row of big baskets, their surly Thai porters. She was in Lisuland again, but how different from her own Lisu friends! Here was no singing, no glad welcome; the Lisu tongue was spoken with a different accent, strange words were used—sometimes she could not fully understand what was said. It was a land in darkness; but the dawn was breaking!

Isobel rejoiced that her comfortable American home had been broken up, and that she had been tossed out again into the back of beyond to help bring the light of a dawn that shall not die away.

★   ★   ★

The special task of Isobel and Edna was to visit a family (their name in Lisu meant Wood, so Isobel always called them the Woods in her letters) who had shown an interest in Christianity. Their hut was not a pleasant place for a call. It was filthily dirty, and Father Wood was the dirtiest old man Isobel had ever seen. He was all bent up with arthritis, but he smiled a welcome and offered his guests the only stool, about two inches high. Both he and his wife smoked opium, and Isobel could not find it in her heart to blame them, seeing the pain he suffered and that his wife, too, was a sick woman. The heathen neighbours crowded into the stuffy hut to see what was going on.

Isobel chatted with them, asking about their health, their family, why they wanted to be Christians. Father Wood had got as far as burning the altar on which he used to sacrifice to the "spirits". Then they suggested he should learn to read, though he was fifty-three, an old man by Lisu standards.

They tried to help him over his health. Would he not wash a little? Wash! That was a queer idea. But certainly he would try, if the teachers thought it would do him good. He even filled a tea-cup with hot water and poured it over his hands, from which the soot ran off in black streams.

They gave him some pills for his arthritic pains, a few every few hours as long as they stayed, for no tribesman will ever obey directions and take the proper number of pills at the proper time. He prefers to swallow the lot at one go. By the end of a week the old man was actually able to walk about—he, who for a long time had not even been able to stand!

That was the beginning of many visits Isobel and Edna paid to Father Wood and the Lisu of Ta-ngo. They paid many more. Young missionaries were settled among the people, and when, two years later, she and John made the trip there were welcoming smiles instead of sullen silence. Father Wood had become a sincere Christian, and even learned to read. From him the circle spread wider and wider among the Lisu of the North Thailand mountains.

Isobel did not see more than the beginning.

12

GOING HOME

STRANGE, that after passing in safety through the dangers of war, brigands, flood, snow and many sicknesses, a piece of stick should bring Isobel's earthly pilgrimage to a close.

It happened on one of those mountain trips. Isobel was struck and bruised by the branch of a tree, while they were walking through woods. She worried a little at the time, but nothing seemed to come of it, and she nearly forgot the small accident. Then, some months later, she slipped and fell, bruising herself again in the same place.

Again nothing seemed to happen. She felt quite well and continued her work for another year. Then trouble showed itself. The Mission doctor advised an operation; a skilful surgeon happened to be in Chiengmai. It was done—but the operation showed that if her life was to be prolonged she must go back to America for treatment.

Isobel was quite calm about it all. From the beginning she had put everything into God's hands, and, somehow, she had the assurance that all would be for the best.

*   *   *

Three weeks after her operation, Isobel's plane landed at Idlewild airport in the U.S.A. She was alone. They had agreed that John was to remain at his post for a year, if the treatment was effective. If she grew worse, he would fly to her at once. Friends were waiting for her, among them her own Kathy, and she was whisked away to the Mission Home, surrounded by love and care, and at once began her treatment at the hospital. Every visit was a painful ordeal, but as it began to take effect and her strength increased she rejoiced that she was still able to work for the Mission. The letters she wrote to John and her friends in Thailand were a real tonic, while the first-hand news she was able to give to her readers in America gathered more and more prayer friends for the work among the tribes.

She knew very well that, though she might have several years to live, the end could not be far away; and before that there was another parting. Kathryn had been accepted as a missionary by the China Inland Mission, and was due to sail in February, 1955. Isobel had arrived home in the previous November—less than four short months with her precious daughter, and then, good-bye. She could not expect to live until Kathryn's first furlough.

No one would have been surprised, and the Mission certainly would have given permission, if Isobel had asked for her daughter's departure to be delayed. She was strongly tempted to do so. It was not just a selfish wish for her own happiness, she told herself. Kathryn's own heart was torn at the thought of leaving her dying mother. But as she prayed and struggled the answer became quite clear; she must hold *nothing* back from Christ. Kathryn must go, as arranged.

A happy Christmas—both her children with her, for

Danny, at school on the other side of the United States, was flown home to be with her. Isobel was getting stronger now, and was able to make plans for a home with Dan when Kathryn should be gone.

"We are not going to give way to grief," she told her friends. "Kathryn understands that we do not love each other any the less because we do not cry over each other. It only weakens us to give way."

"Mummy, I didn't shed a tear when the ship pulled out," Kathryn wrote in a letter posted at Halifax on the outward voyage. That was something of a triumph, for Kathryn was as warm-hearted and affectionate as her mother.

*　　*　　*

Isobel was no idle invalid! All her missionary life her letters had been a joy and inspiration to those at home, and very wisely when the trouble in China started she had seen to it that all her notes and papers were sent away. Now she used her great gift of writing to gather her stored experiences into book form. Many a young man or woman has been helped and guided through the difficulties and bewilderment of trying to find God's truth by her book, *By Searching*, which tells about her girlhood; and in two later books she wrote of a missionary's life just as it is, with all its discouragements and pitfalls as well as its triumphs. Rich in wisdom, she poured it all out.

That summer she was strong enough to travel and do some speaking at camps and conferences. And John came home! The Mission had felt that husband and wife should

have some time together while Isobel was still compara-
tively well, and the two of them stood side by side at two
autumn conferences.

Well and pretty as Isobel looked, she knew that her
trouble was progressing. Another operation was suggested.
Isobel said:

"I'm not going to have it. It wouldn't be a cure, just
arrest the trouble temporarily and prolong my life. As it
is, I'm an expense to the Mission and keeping John from
going back to the field work."

That was the wrong way to look at it, and her friends
told her so. She was doing most valuable work by her
writing, work that would endure for many years, and she
owed it to them to continue as long as she could. So she
consented, the operation took place, and her life on earth
was lengthened by a few more months.

She wrote to her brother: "Just because I am sick
people value what I write twice as much as they did
before, so I feel I am still earning my way, so to speak.
The Mission would support me in any case, but it is a
very happy thing to me to be able to do something of
value."

Weakness and pain increased, but she kept on writing—
not only for home readers, but tracts in the Lisu language
for her dear Lisu far away. Happy news came. Kathryn
was engaged to a young missionary well known to John
and Isobel, a former comrade on the field. How right the
mother had been to let the daughter go!

The pen was too heavy to hold now. Isobel lay waiting
for the home call, weak, suffering, but confident. Just one
thing more she wished for, and it came: Kathryn's

wedding! Photographs were sent by air, and arrived in time for her to rejoice over them. Daughter Kathryn was launched in a life of service, with a good husband at her side. Son Danny was in the loving care of friends; better still, in the loving care of the Lord his mother served and trusted.

On March 20, 1957, alone with John, the gates opened for Isobel Kuhn.

"If ever I was near heaven," John said afterwards, "and if ever I was conscious that death had lost its sting, it was then."